MW01102141

COUNTRIES IN THE NEWS

IRAN

Kieran Walsh

Rourke
Publishing LLC
Vero Beach, Florida 32964

www.rourkepublishing.com

The country's flag is correct at the time of going to press.

PHOTO CREDITS:
All images © Peter Langer Associated Media Group

Title page: A mosque in Kermanshah

Editor: Frank Sloan

Cover and interior design by Nicola Stratford

Library of Congress Cataloging-in-Publication Data

Walsh, Kieran.
 Iran / Kieran Walsh.
    p. cm. — (Countries in the news)
Includes bibliographical references and index.
Contents: Welcome to Iran — The people — Life in Iran — School and sports — Food and holidays — The future — Fast facts — The Muslim world.
 ISBN 1-58952-677-5
 1. Iran—Juvenile literature. [1. Iran.] I. Title. II. Series: Walsh Kieran. Countries in the news.
 DS254.75.W354 2003
 955—dc21
                                         2003005672

Printed in the USA
CG/CG

TABLE OF CONTENTS

WELCOME TO
IRAN

Iran is a very large country in the western part of Asia. For many years, the land was called Persia. In 1935 it became known as Iran. Long ago, the Persian Empire was in the middle of the great trade routes that ran from east to west.

The village of Alamout in the Alborz Mountains

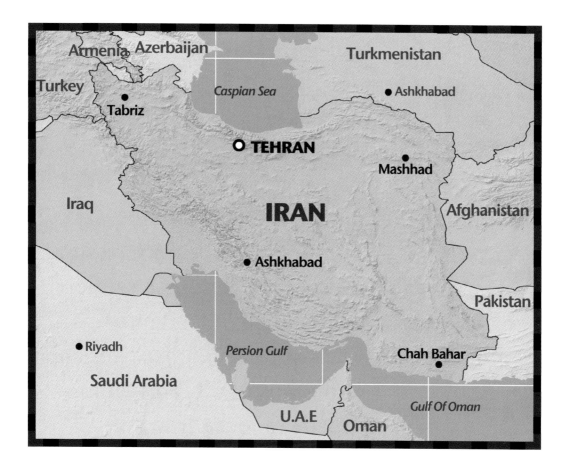

The country is about 1,200 miles (1,930 kilometers) across at its widest point. Iran is about the size of the states of California, New Mexico, Arizona, and Texas combined.

Iran has two major mountain chains. One group of mountains runs east to west across the top of the country, and another runs north to south in the west. The Caspian Sea is at the north on the border with Russia. It is the largest **landlocked** body of water in the world.

About one sixth of Iran is desert. Only a small amount of the land in Iran can be used for farming. Iran is also subject to big earthquakes. The country has deserts, plains, and mountains. Because of this, the weather changes depending on the kind of land.

Underneath much of the land there are huge amounts of oil. This oil has made modern Iran an important country.

Isfahan is another well-known city in Iran. It has many old palaces, **minarets**, and **mosques**.

> **!** Tehran is the nation's capital and its largest city. A busy place, Tehran is a blend of ancient buildings and many new ones. Bazaars are next to modern hotels and office buildings. There is a great deal of traffic in Tehran.

Azadi Square in Tehran

THE PEOPLE

People who live in Iran are known as Iranians. More than half of these people are farmers, many of whom live in small villages. There may be as many as 50,000 small villages scattered over Iran. Probably less than half of Iranians live in cities.

An Iranian woman leads her donkey among goats in a small village.

A woman reads the Koran at a service in Tehran.

About 90% of Iranians are Muslims. This means they follow the religion of Islam. Some are advanced and **liberal**. They are known as **Sunni**. Many Muslims are **conservative**. They are known as **Shiite**. Sometimes these people are known as **fundamentalists**. Iran is one of the few Muslim countries where there are more Shiite than Sunni Muslims.

Because many Iranians are farmers, water is important to them. Many years ago, Persians built dams so they could get water to grow crops. Today there are many new dams that provide **irrigation**.

In the cities, many Iranians work in industry. Many are involved in the textile and carpet business. Some Iranians work for the government.

A carpet worker weaves a Persian rug in a small village.

LIFE IN
IRAN

Families are important in Iran. Many family members may live together. In larger cities, these people may be crowded into small apartments.

In the cities most men dress in western clothes. So do many of the women. But in small villages, women may cover their faces and bodies when they go out in public.

A street vendor displays his goods near a shrine in Mashhad.

Young people fish in a country stream.

SCHOOL AND SPORTS

Education is poor in Iran. Where they exist, schools are free. Some schools, particularly in small villages, may go only as far as Grades 2 or 4. Children are supposed to go to elementary school for at least six years. Many girls do not even attend schools. More and more, especially in the cities, schools are improving and providing classes through high school. There are also many new colleges and universities in Iran.

! Soccer is a popular sport in Iran. So is **alak do lak**. This is a traditional game in which a bat is used to hit a small piece of wood. Iranians like many other games and sports, and they also enjoy hunting.

Young women walk outdoors in Shiraz.

FOOD AND HOLIDAYS

Iranians eat a lot of wheat and rice. They also add lamb on many occasions, and often yogurt accompanies many meals. Tea is very popular, and is served at almost all meals. Tea is also considered a welcoming drink for visitors.

As in most Muslim countries, **Ramadan** is the most important holiday. Muslims observe the month-long period with **fasting** during the day. At the end of Ramadan, the fasting is over, and people celebrate **Id ul Fitr**, a time of feasting and exchanging presents. Another important holiday in Iran is **No-Ruz**. This is the first day of the Muslim New Year.

Young and old share a meal in Mashhad.

In Mashhad, modern cars and buses whiz past the Imam Rezah Shrine.

THE FUTURE

For many years in the 20th century, Iran was a **monarchy** ruled by a group of **shahs**. These shahs wanted to modernize Iran, and they sometimes achieved good results. But many people were unhappy. In 1979 conservatives rose up and formed an Islamic **republic**. Many people went back to earlier, less modern, beliefs.

Oil has been a great help to Iranians. Much of the money that comes in from the sale of oil to other countries has been used to help modernize agriculture.

Education has also been greatly improved.

As the 21st century begins, Iran is trying hard to become part of the modern world.

FAST FACTS

Area: 631,700 square miles
(1,636,000 square kilometers)

Borders: Turkey, Iraq, Armenia, Azerbaijan,
Turkmenistan, Afghanistan, Pakistan

Population: 66,622,704
Monetary Unit: rial

Largest Cities: Tehran (7,038,000);
Isfahan (1,381,000)
Government: Islamic republic

Religion: Shiite Muslim (89%); Sunni Muslim (10%)
Crops: grains, rice, fruits, nuts

Natural Resources: chromium, coal, oil, gas
Major Industries: oil, textiles, cement

THE MUSLIM WORLD

There are more than 1,200,000,000 Muslims in the world. Almost two thirds of them live in Asia and Africa. There are two major groups of Muslims: 16% of them are Shiite and 83% are known as Sunni. In Iran, however, there are many more Shiites than Sunnis.

Muslims follow the Islam religion. The word "Islam" means submission to one God. They call God Allah.

The religion began around AD 610 when Muhammad became known as a prophet. He wrote down his teachings in a holy book called the Koran. Muslims are required to pray five times a day.

GLOSSARY

alak do lak (AH LACK DO LACK) — a traditional game played in Iran

conservative (cuhn SUHR vet iv) — someone who believes in traditional methods or views

fasting (FAST ing) — giving up certain foods, usually for religious reasons

fundamentalists (fun duh MENT uh lists) — people who have strict beliefs

Id ul Fitr (ID UHL FIT ur) — a holiday celebrated at the end of Ramadan

irrigation (ir uh GAY shun) — a system that provides water for growing crops

landlocked (LAND LOCKD) — without access to any bodies of water

liberal (LIB uh ruhl) — one who is open-minded and not strict

minarets (min uh RETZ) — towers attached to mosques

monarchy (MON ahr kee) — a country ruled by a king or queen

mosques (MOSKS) — Muslim places of worship

No-Ruz (NOH ROOZ) — the first day of the Muslim new year

Ramadan (RAM uh DAN) — the ninth month of the Muslim year and a time of fasting

republic (ree PUB lick) — a political unit in which the leader has been elected

shahs (SHA WZ) — a series of kinglike Iranian leaders

Shiite (SHEE ITE) — a sect of Muslims, basically conservative

Sunni (SOO NEE) — a sect of Muslims, known for being liberal

FURTHER READING

Find out more about Iran with these helpful books:

- Italia, Bob. *Iran.* Checkerboard Library, 2002.
- Marchant, Kerena. *Muslim Festival Tales.* Raintree Steck Vaughn, 2001.
- Moritz, Patricia. *Dropping in on Iran.* Rourke Publishing, 2001
- Schemenauer, Elma. *Iran.* Child's World, 2000.
- Yip, Dora, and Maria O'Shea. *Welcome to Iran.* Gareth Stevens, 2001.

WEBSITES TO VISIT

- www.netiran.com/
- www.daftar.org/default _eng.htm

INDEX

About the Author

Kieran Walsh is a writer of children's nonfiction books, primarily on historical and social studies topics. A graduate of Manhattan College, in Riverdale, NY, his degree is in Communications. Walsh has been involved in the children's book field as editor, proofreader, and illustrator as well as author.